The Waterman/Harewood Piano Series

Recital Repertoire Book Two

Sonatas and Sonatinas

selected and edited by

Fanny Waterman

and

Marion Harewood

Faber Music Limited
London

THE CLASSICAL SONATA

A Sonata or Sonatina (a smaller-scale Sonata) is normally a work for solo instruments in two, three or four movements, the first of which is in what is known as 'sonata form'. It was in the second half of the eighteenth century that this form evolved, notably in the works of C. P. E. Bach and Haydn. Previously the term Sonata could refer to a variety of musical compositions: it could be applied to a piece of purely instrumental music (*sonare* – to sound) as opposed to a vocal composition or Cantata (*cantare* – to sing). It could be applied to a suite of movements meant to be played as a single work, or, as in Domenico Scarlatti's harpsichord sonatas, to a single movement in two sections (binary form).

The works in this volume follow the pattern of the classical Sonata as developed by Haydn, Mozart and Beethoven, a pattern which you will find in the classical symphony, string quartet, and in a modified form in the classical concerto.

THE FIRST MOVEMENT is in sonata form. This basic structure consists of an Exposition moving from the tonic key to the dominant key, a Development passing through a wide range of keys, and a Recapitulation entirely in the tonic. Sometimes, as in the Beethoven Sonata in this volume, the movement starts with a slow introduction.

The Exposition has two main parts. The First Subject, in the tonic key, usually carries the main musical weight of the movement; it is connected by a bridge passage to the Second Subject, which is often in a contrasting mood and in a key which is different but closely related. Sometimes further subsidiary themes are introduced, and the Exposition generally ends in the dominant key, often at a double bar.

In the Development the themes can be elaborated, telescoped or broken into melodic or rhythmic patterns. The music modulates through several keys before returning to the tonic for the Recapitulation. Here the music of the Exposition is repeated, but with both the subjects now in the main key. The movement sometimes ends with an extended Coda or tail-piece – usually a brilliant passage to end the movement with a flourish.

It is the change of keys in sonata form which is most important. In the Czerny Sonatina the Recapitulation at bar 84 starts not with the music from the beginning of the Exposition, but with the Second Subject (c.f. bar 15), but the basic principle is still of an Exposition moving from tonic to dominant, the Recapitulation remaining in the tonic. The same is true in the Kuhlau Sonatina when the Recapitulation (bar 36) starts half way through the First Subject (c.f. bar 9).

Where there are more than two movements THE SECOND MOVEMENT is contrasted in tempo, mood and key and is usually of a lyrical character. It can be in the form of an Aria, a set of Variations or even modified sonata form. Some Sonatas also include a MINUET or SCHERZO movement, with a central Trio section.

LAST MOVEMENTS vary in style and form. Their function is to balance the first movement, but the content is usually of a lighter character. They can be planned in a variety of ways, depending on the preceding movements. Frequently they are in the form of a Rondo, or a set of Variations or a simplified sonata form.

This shape of the classical sonata was perfected by Haydn, Mozart and the young Beethoven. In this volume it is seen in the Beethoven Sonata. The other Sonatas and Sonatinas (apart from the Schumann Children's Sonata) are shorter and more compressed with just a first and a last movement. Later in his life Beethoven used the structure more loosely to enable him to give freer expression to his musical ideas. The Romantic composers of the later nineteenth century altered the form further, and Schumann's Children's Sonata, for example, bears little resemblance to the classical form of the earlier Viennese masters. Composers today use the word Sonata in its original meaning of a substantial composition for solo instruments.

F.W.
M.H.

Sonatina

Op. 36, No. 6

MUZIO CLEMENTI
(1752–1832)

p espress.
fz
pp
cresc.
f
p
cresc.
ff

cresc.
cresc.
dim.
dolce

poco fz
poco fz
poco fz
cresc.
f
ff
fz
mf
cresc.
ff
p espress.

fz
cresc.
f
p
cresc.
ff

6
RONDO
Allegretto spiritoso
dim.
R.H. 2nd finger: curve it!
Oct. 27th
Scales: D & G in Tenths (p. 9 & 6)
Exercise (not too strenuously...)
Keep 3rd finger above or on G all the time.
L.H.
M.S.

Fine
ff
p
f
ff
dim.

rhythm
Keep 5th on, but keep L.H. light.
light & lyrical
staccato practice
busy & loud
sub. p
*Start on upper note (B)
tr
Smooth
Count!
Da Capo

Sonatina

Op. 55, No. 3

FRIEDRICH KUHLAU
(1786–1832)

p
pp
Short rest!!
cresc.
Count: 6 7 8 | 1 2 3 4
f
dim.
p
f
f
p scherzando

cresc.
f
Interrupted Cadence
A minor, not C
Fourth finger independent of 3rd
f

Allegretto grazioso
p
f
cresc.
dim.
1.
2.
mf giocoso

smorz.
cresc.
f
mf
più f
f
dim.
p
poco rit.
a tempo

cresc.
dim.

Sonatina
Op.163 No.2

CARL CZERNY
(1791–1857)

Allegro moderato

cresc.
f
ff
p
mf
f

cresc.
p
pp
cresc.
f
dim.
rit.
a tempo
p

cresc.
f
ff
Rondo
Allegretto vivace
p giocoso

mf
p
mf
p
cresc.
sf
sf
p

8
8
cresc.
f
sf
sf
p grazioso
dolce

cresc.
f
p
cresc.
p
cresc.
f
p
cresc.
f

a tempo
p
mf
p
mf
p
cresc.
8
f

sf
sf
p
8
8
8
cresc.
f
sf
sf
ff

Dedicated to Princess Marie Esterhazy

Sonata

Hob. XVI/40

JOSEPH HAYDN
(1732–1809)

Work on left hand security

Ties!
staccato practice
C note
Ped.

fz
f
p
f
p
fz
fz
fz
1.
mf
2.
p
p
cresc.
f
ffz
Pick out 'skeleton' notes mark
ffz
fz
fz
p
f
f
accents. Practise slowly & make 5th finger work independently.

as fast as poss.
8 cut out the fine details
dim.

Important fingering! Practise broken chords (G major).
Presto
Count!
Wait!

tr
ffz
p
legato!
r.h.
f

don't slow down

mf legato

p

f

p

f

p

4 equal ♪s.

All needed

fz
tr
p
tr
cresc.
f

scherzando
leggiero

Sonata
K. 547a

WOLFGANG AMADEUS MOZART
(1756–1791)

tr
mp
tr
f
mf
f
tr
mf
f
tr
f

cresc.

f
dim.
mf
cresc.
f
p dolce
f
p dolce
f
f
f

Allegretto
p
mf
f
p

Sonata

Composed in 1783
(aged 13)

LUDWIG VAN BEETHOVEN
(1770–1827)

f
pp
f
p
pp
f
ff

ff
p
ff
Larghetto maestoso
f
p
f
p
f
ff
tr
Allegro assai
ff
p

Andante
p cantabile
f
p
tr
cresc.

f
p

Presto
p
f
mf
cresc.
f

mf
cresc.
f
f
f
f
p
f
p
cresc.
f

pp
p
cresc.
f
p
cresc.
f
f

f
p
cresc.
ff

54
Exercise for constructively disordered fingering...
Sonata for Children
(for Julien)
Op. 118 No. 1
1. Allegro
ROBERT SCHUMANN
(1810–1856)
Lebhaft (Lively) ♩ =92
cresc.

cresc.
fp
cresc.

2. Theme and Variations

dolce
leggiero
p
zurückhaltend
(rit.)
im Takt
(a tempo)
Etwas langsamer
(A little slower)
espress.
pp

3. Doll's Lullaby

cresc.
f
cresc.
f
p
zurückhaltend
(rit.)
im Takt
(a tempo)

4. Rondoletto

one two three
poco rit.
a tempo
ritard.
a tempo
una corda

p
tre corde
pp
p